Attingham Park
Shropshire

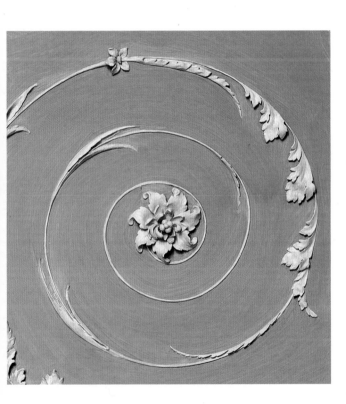

National Trust

A Story of Love and Neglect

Only five generations of Berwicks lived at Attingham, but theirs was an impressive and enduring legacy.

Changing fortunes

The Berwicks left a fine Georgian mansion with intricate decoration, Regency furniture and art, splendid stables and a walled garden as well as a deer park, all set in a 4,000-acre estate in the fertile valley of the River Severn. But these physical structures are only part of the story – Attingham has been the setting for astutely accumulated fortunes, flamboyant overspending and financial ruin. It is a story of love and neglect, of changing fortunes, revival and rediscovery.

Politics and money

Shrewd investment, trade and clever political manoeuvring by the earlier Hill family members from the 1500s onwards meant that Noel Hill, who became the 1st Lord Berwick, had ample funds to commission an impressive new house and stables in 1782 on his inherited country estate.

Politics also shaped the lives of the 1st and 3rd Lords Berwick who were MPs for Shrewsbury. This brought them status and influence in Shropshire and nearby counties. But politics was a costly business in the Georgian period and elections made heavy demands on the family fortune.

Attingham Hall, commissioned in 1782 for Noel Hill, 1st Lord Berwick, was a mark of his status and wealth but he never lived to see it finished

The Italian connection

There is a strong Italian thread running through the Attingham story. The 2nd Lord Berwick spent two years in Italy on his Grand Tour and brought back paintings, sculpture and antiquities to adorn Attingham's principal rooms. William, 3rd Lord Berwick, lived in Italy for 28 years as a British diplomat and, on his return, lavished some of his Italianate tastes on Attingham. Teresa Hulton, wife of Thomas, the 8th Lord Berwick, grew up in Venice, and was the last of the family to bring the artistic life of Italy to rural Shropshire.

Above The Drawing Room contains paintings and furniture brought back from Italy by the 2nd and 3rd Lords Berwick and a portrait of Teresa, wife of the 8th Lord Berwick who was born and raised in Italy

Tricks and illusions

Attingham was built to impress and amaze, but not everything is as it appears. Tiles resemble bricks, painted bricks resemble stone, while fake marble, false doors and clever paintwork are all designed to deceive the eye. This wasn't cheating or an attempt at economy, but a demonstration of the latest fashions in interior design.

Spenders, Savers and Saviours

Attingham has seen times of expansion and decline, of careful repair and enforced economies, and now, under the care of the National Trust, of innovation and restoration.

Noel Hill was the man who commissioned Attingham Hall and stables. Energetic and pragmatic he was MP for Shrewsbury. As well as his existing family fortune, Noel added further status to the family name by astutely supporting Prime Minister William Pitt the Younger in his reorganisation of the East India Company. Noel was given a title in 1784, becoming the 1st Baron Berwick and took the motto QUI UTI SCIT EI BONA 'Let wealth be his who knows its use', which turned out to be quite ironic for this family.

Noel already owned Tern Hall, the original house on the site, and commissioned George Steuart, a Scottish architect, to design a new home for his wife Anne and their six children. They decided to build it around Tern Hall, enclosing and extending it in all directions, creating a large new mansion called Attingham Hall.

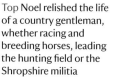

Top Noel relished the life of a country gentleman, whether racing and breeding horses, leading the hunting field or the Shropshire militia

Middle Anne with her son Thomas. A devoted mother, she left personal keepsakes to each of her six children

Above The Hills' three daughters, Henrietta, Anne and Amelia, all highly accomplished musicians

Left View of Tern Hall, 1775. Tern Hall was integrated into the new Attingham Hall

Noel and Anne Hill, 1st Lord and Lady Berwick: the creators of Attingham

A family home

Noel and Anne had three boys and three girls. They were the only Hill family children ever to be brought up at Attingham. All three sons, Thomas, William and Richard, inherited Attingham becoming the 2nd, 3rd and 4th Lords Berwick. Their sisters, Henrietta, Anne and Amelia, would have been educated in music, languages and the arts. Henrietta, the eldest was an accomplished musician and played the satinwood gilded organ now in the Picture Gallery. After Noel's sudden death in 1789, the three sisters travelled to Naples with their mother, joining their brother Thomas, who was on his Grand Tour. Their mother stayed in Italy until she died in 1797, not only because the Napoleonic Wars made European travel difficult, but also because she wasn't left sufficiently wealthy to keep an independent establishment in London, despite the vast fortune Thomas inherited.

Two halves of a whole

Noel and Anne may have married for love as Noel's family did not approve of the match. The design of their new house adopted the French fashion of a masculine and a feminine side in terms of decoration. The Drawing Room, Sultana Room, East Ante Room and Boudoir form the feminine side with exquisite gilding and beautifully painted flowers, birds and Cupid's arrows. The Dining Room, Inner Library, West Ante Room and Octagon Room make up the masculine side and contain strong colours, family portraits and other manly objects. The Boudoir (right) and Octagon rooms are the most private rooms on the *piano nobile*, the main level of the house.

Thomas and Sophia, 2nd Lord and Lady Berwick: big spenders in an extravagant age

Thomas was a man of fashionable taste and a passionate collector of paintings, sculptures and books. He was also committed to Attingham, completing and improving the mansion and its surrounding landscape; he increased the acreage of the estate by a third. However, his extravagant purchases – he admitted to his brother that he couldn't 'abstain from Building and Picture buying' – coupled with his wife's frivolous spending, brought Attingham to financial ruin in 1827.

Grand Tour souvenirs

Thomas inherited Attingham in 1789 at the age of 18, when he was studying at Cambridge. As was fashionable among the young elite, he set off on a Grand Tour of Italy. Like many of his contemporaries, he travelled to Italy to see the countryside, its archaeology and classical architecture. He purchased antiquities and commissioned sculpture and paintings by the famous artists. His tutor made a model of Mount Vesuvius which remained at Attingham until 1913. When Thomas returned home in 1794 with his souvenirs, he set about completing the decoration of the mansion and commissioned the architect, John Nash, to design a new picture gallery to display his growing art collection.

The Grand Tour
In the 1700s, when Britain was the wealthiest nation in the world, privileged young Englishmen spent several years travelling Europe. It was a cultural experience, improving their languages and knowledge of art and architecture – an early version of the 'Gap Year'. They visited major cities, renting an apartment or villa for months, presenting letters of introduction to family contacts. This portrait of Thomas in his early twenties in historic fancy dress, was painted by Angelica Kauffman when he was visiting Rome.

Courting a courtesan

Thomas met his future wife, Sophia, in London and apparently drove up and down in his splendid carriage, a curricle, to attract her attention. Her sister, the 'kiss-and-tell' writer Harriette Wilson, later wrote: 'Sophia has a new conquest of an elderly gentleman, in a curricle with a crest on it'. Like some of her sisters, Sophia was a courtesan (a mistress) and lived in Mayfair amongst the aristocracy. The 41-year-old Lord Berwick continued to pursue her until she eventually agreed to marry him in 1812.

Marriage and money

Sophia, a tradesman's daughter, gained great wealth through her marriage, but was she truly happy? Thomas and Sophia were big spenders and Sophia's sister, Harriette Wilson, herself an infamous courtesan, commented that: 'Sophia, having the command of more guineas than ever she had expected to have pence, did nothing, from morning till night, but throw them away'. Lord Berwick had always spent lavishly and eventually, Attingham's contents were put up for sale in 1827 and again in 1829 to pay the creditors.

Shortly before the auctions, Lord and Lady Berwick moved to Italy. Thomas died in 1832, just three years after the second auction. Sophia later returned to England to live in Leamington Spa where she died aged 81 in 1875.

Top *The Excavations at Pompeii*, by Jacob Philipp Hackert, 1799 purchased by Thomas, 2nd Lord Berwick. When Hackert painted this picture the uncovering and recording of Classical remains in Italy, Greece and Egypt was of interest to wealthy young men such as Lord Berwick

Above This intricate music box, still in working order, is believed to have been given as a gift from Thomas to Sophia

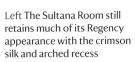

Left The Sultana Room still retains much of its Regency appearance with the crimson silk and arched recess

William, 3rd Lord Berwick: 'an Excellent diplomat'

working in Italy as a diplomat. Like his father and elder brother, he added another layer to Attingham's story, with strong Italian elements. The mansion's interiors reflect his taste, with white and gilded Italian furniture from the Palazzo Belvedere, the home of Caroline Murat, Napoleon's sister, as well as paintings, impressive silver and French porcelain.

Lost bonnets and passports

Like many younger sons of the British aristocracy, William went into the diplomatic service. He spent much of his career in Italy as British Envoy. He modestly, and perhaps honestly, described his diplomatic role as being largely concerned with 'losses of Bonnets & Gowns, cruel Custom House officers or the want of Passports'. However he was a natural *bon viveur* and enjoyed a lavish lifestyle, wining and dining the great and the good. One of the people he entertained was the poet Lord Byron, who was travelling through Italy to Greece. Byron described William as 'the only one of the diplomatists whom I ever knew who really is Excellent'.

An unexpected inheritance

William never married. Although he and his Italian mistress had children, they could not inherit Attingham as they were illegitimate. When William died in 1842, aged 69, Attingham passed to his younger brother, Richard, a 68-year-old Shropshire rector who had never expected to inherit Attingham.

When Thomas, 2nd Lord Berwick, had to auction most of Attingham's goods to pay his creditors, his younger brothers, William and Richard, tried to buy some of the furniture and family paintings. William also leased Attingham from Thomas, providing vital income. In the 1830s, William brought to Attingham his dazzling collection of Italian furniture and art accumulated during his 28 years living and

Left William, 3rd Lord Berwick, rescued Attingham after his brother's financial ruin. He collected many of the paintings and furniture now at Attingham while he was living in Italy

Opposite The white and gilded furniture in the Drawing Room imported from Italy, including a daybed that may have belonged to Caroline Murat, Napoleon's sister

A flood of letters

The Hon. William Hill, later 3rd Lord Berwick, bought what he could at the 1827 sale, dispatching a flood of distraught letters to his younger brother Richard and his agents. 'They must acquire the family portraits, and some of the furniture (not the showy stuff) and paintings, especially the two Hackerts.'

The Lake of Avernus pictured here was one of the paintings by Jacob Philipp Hackert (1737–1807) bought by Thomas in Italy and by William at the 1827 auction.

Perks of the job

As a high ranking diplomat, William had to entertain important dignitaries and high-ranking travelling British citizens. He was supplied with 5,833 ounces of silver and 1,066 ounces of gold, which he had made into fabulous silver-gilt and silver tableware by Paul Storr, London's finest silversmith in the early 1800s. Although due to be 'returned on demand', William somehow retained all this silver and goldware when he returned to live at Attingham. It may have been part of a 'deal' to encourage William to leave his post in Naples to make way for Lord Palmerston's nephew.

4th, 5th, 6th and 7th Lords Berwick

Richard, 4th Lord Berwick: a county cleric

Richard, 4th Lord Berwick, was Rector of Berrington, on the Attingham estate. As the third son, he enjoyed the life of a country gentleman, and built Berrington Rectory where he lived with his wife and children. Like his brothers, he also enjoyed spending money and Thomas described him as 'so very idle and extravagant of his wife, indolent and ignorant of management.' He had a large family but struggled financially to support them. His wife, Frances, had died by the time he gained the title and it was said that he didn't entertain but 'swallowed more wine than any other man in the County'.

Richard, 5th Lord Berwick: a country squire

The eldest son of the 4th Lord Berwick, another Richard, inherited Attingham in 1848. As a young man he had spent time in Italy with his uncle, William. His stewardship of Attingham marked the end of the estate's flamboyant Georgian era and the start of a more careful, early Victorian period. Through astute management he cleared the estate's inherited debts, and in 1856 commissioned extensive repairs and alterations to the mansion, removing what remained of the original family home, Tern Hall. He modernised the estate's agriculture, building model farms and establishing an internationally famous herd of Hereford cattle. Richard chose to live at Cronkhill, a stylish villa designed by John Nash on the Attingham estate. Quiet but resourceful, he was innovative and entrepreneurial, inventing the Cronkhill rifle and creating flutes and clarinets.

Above Richard, 5th Lord Berwick

Below left Richard, 4th Lord Berwick

Below right Frances, wife of the 4th Lord Berwick, died before he gained the title and therefore never became Lady Berwick but her two eldest sons both inherited in turn

Model farms

Richard, 5th Lord Berwick, followed the trend among many Victorian landowners in building 'model farms' which incorporated recent improvements in agricultural techniques, efficiency and layout to make farming more profitable. Richard's model farms were built in brick and designed to be both aesthetic and functional. His foresight gave the estate the economic strength and stability to withstand the national downturn in agriculture in the 1880s and 1890s.

William, 6th Lord Berwick: a serving soldier

William, Richard's younger brother, inherited Attingham when he was nearly 60 years old. A colonel in the army, he never married and never lived permanently at Attingham, choosing to live at Springfield House near Shrewsbury, then part of the Attingham estate. He entertained at Attingham occasionally, probably bringing his servants from Springfield over for the event. The 1871 census records that he had seventeen live-in servants – an extensive household, even for Victorian times. William took interest in the estate and bought and sold some of the paintings. He was a cautious man who helped to consolidate Attingham in the Victorian period.

Richard and Ellen, 7th Lord and Lady Berwick: a keen yachtsman with financial problems

Richard was one of the 6th Lord Berwick's twin nephews. As a young man he had a short spell in the Army, bought a yacht, the 'Clio', and, to the disapproval of high society, married Ellen Nystrom who came from a lower social class. It was an unsuccessful marriage and the couple did not live together on a permanent basis. After inheriting the title in 1882, Richard visited Attingham to shoot. He had financial problems throughout his adult life and, in contravention of the Will of the 5th Lord Berwick, he sold family heirlooms. He died in 1897 but his wife, Ellen, survived him by nearly 30 years and was fondly regarded by the 8th Lord and Lady Berwick.

Above left William, 6th Lord Berwick

Above centre The 7th Lord and Lady Berwick (far right) with a shooting party at Cronkhill

Above right Richard, 7th Lord Berwick

Thomas and Teresa, 8th Lord and Lady Berwick: the saviours of Attingham

In 1897 Thomas became the last Lord Berwick to inherit Attingham. After studying at Cambridge, he entered the diplomatic service and was sent to Paris in 1903, a time of great change and disruption in Europe. In Paris Thomas developed a passion for French decorative arts and began buying appropriate paintings, sculptures, furniture and textiles for Attingham.

From the time of his inheritance, Thomas made improvements to Attingham. Electricity was installed using a steam engine to generate power, the water supply was upgraded to make it suitable for tenants and in 1912 proposals were made for a heating system, Lord Berwick also carried out work on the estate's tenant farms. To fund these works, land was sold to ensure the survival of the core part of Attingham.

Artistic circles

In 1919 Thomas married Teresa Hulton whom he had met before the outbreak of the First World War. During the war years, Lord Berwick had been based in Northumberland, Paris and northern Italy while Teresa served as a Red Cross nurse on the Italian front line. Her father, William Hulton, was a painter whose artist friends included Walter Sickert and John Singer Sargent. Teresa's mother was half-Italian, and their family life in Venice was cultured and lively, at the heart of literary and artistic communities. Lord and Lady Berwick moved into Cronkhill after their honeymoon but made Attingham their home in 1921 when they could not find tenants for the large house.

A new lease of life

When Thomas and Teresa moved into the mansion it was in a poor state. It had been let since 1901 to Major Atherley and from 1913 to the Dutch-American Van Bergen family. During the First World War, part of the house had been used as a hospital for wounded soldiers. The main state rooms had become worn which led the Berwicks to carry out careful repairs on a limited budget. Thomas had already bought French furniture and silk damasks and he sought out suitable additions to the collection, such as the portrait of Caroline Murat and two statues in the style of Canova in the Drawing Room.

Wartime use

During the Second World War, the staff and pupils of Edgbaston Church of England Girls' School were evacuated to Attingham. Towards the end of the war it was home to the Women's Auxiliary Air Force. The 8th Lord and Lady Berwick remained at Attingham throughout the war, occupying a few rooms on the east side. James Lees-Milne, the National Trust Secretary in the late 1930s and 40s, visited them to discuss the future of Attingham. After his visit he wrote, 'The Berwicks live at Attingham in the utmost simplicity, out of necessity.'

Ensuring Attingham's future

In 1937 Thomas began negotiating with the National Trust about the future of Attingham. In his shy and modest manner he wrote that he had 'some pride in this house...having been owner of the Attingham estate since Nov 1897, nearly 50 years....'

Thomas gifted Attingham to the National Trust and it remains today one of the most generous bequests the Trust has ever received. His Memorandum of Wishes stated that it should be shown as 'a good example of Eighteenth Century Architecture with such contents in the principal rooms as a nobleman of that period would have had'. Thomas and Teresa's vision for Attingham, and their combined love and knowledge of fine and decorative arts, ensured the preservation of one of the most complete late Georgian country house estates in England.

Opposite The 8th Lord and Lady Berwick reading in the Picture Gallery

Above Statue of Venus purchased by the 8th Lord Berwick

Right Teresa, wife of the 8th Lord Berwick salvaged old trimmings and kept them in shoeboxes for repair

Far right The 8th Lord and Lady Berwick had no children but secured Attingham's future with the National Trust

The Adult Education College: a new age

Teresa, wife of the 8th Lord Berwick, spent her married life and widowhood at Attingham. When her husband died in 1947, she continued to live in the house and occupy her rooms. Before Thomas' death, it was arranged that much of the mansion would be leased to Shropshire County Council for use as an adult education college. Lady Berwick, therefore, shared the house with the National Trust and the college.

The college was led by the charismatic, Sir George Trevelyan. As warden, he directed the college with foresight, inspiration and innovation during the 1950s and 1960s. Attingham became a leading college for life-long learning with an eclectic programme of residential courses covering topics such as costume, music, poetry, theatre, astrology, Christian philosophy and starting a farm.

Changes in the mansion

College use inevitably required some internal structural changes. The suite of upper rooms lavishly decorated in the early 1800s for Sophia, wife of the 2nd Lord Berwick, was partitioned to make bathrooms and dormitories. Student accommodation was also created at the back of the house and the ceiling of the Victorian kitchen was lowered to create rooms above. The Dining Room became a lecture theatre and the Octagon Room became Sir George Trevelyan's office.

Right Folk-dancing lesson, 1948

National Trust

Between the 1950s and 70s, the mansion was largely occupied as a college, the walled garden was let to a nurseryman and the service rooms at the back of the mansion were almost derelict. In the 1980s the National Trust started a programme of building work to repair the roofs and create space for their regional office. Detailed research started then too, sorting through estate records and archives to find out more about the history of the mansion and its collections, the grounds, parkland and estate as well as the people who had lived and worked at Attingham.

Fascinating stories

Staff and volunteers have spent thousands of hours searching through records and archive materials. Their painstaking work has unearthed fascinating treasures – letters from the 1st Lord Berwick to his sons, catalogues for the 1827 and 1829 sales held to pay off the 2nd Lord Berwick's debts, records of journeys made by servants and their annual wages, details of the 3rd Lord Berwick's diplomatic postings and fascinating letters between the 8th Lord and Lady Berwick. Slowly but surely, the lives of the people who have lived at Attingham are being revealed. Visitors to Attingham are rediscovering the intriguing stories of the mansion and its occupants and are joining the debate about the conservation and restoration of this inspirational Georgian country estate.

Left The 1827 sale catalogue offers a window into the contents of Attingham Hall during the extravagant time of the 2nd Lord Berwick

Right Letters in the Attingham archive reveal fascinating stories

ATTINGHAM HALL,
NEAR SHREWSBURY, IN THE COUNTY OF SALOP.
SUPERB FURNITURE:
COSTLY SERVICE OF SILVER AND GILT PLATE;
CELLARS OF FINE OLD WINES;
VALUABLE LIBRARY OF BOOKS;
FINE PAINTINGS, AND SCULPTURES IN MARBLE.
A CATALOGUE
OF THE SUPERB
FURNITURE,
Designed and Executed in the first style of Elegance and Fashion, by one of the principal Manufacturers in London;
NOBLE PIER & CHIMNEY GLASSES; SPLENDID CUT GLASS LUSTRES & CHANDELIERS;
BRILLIANT-TONED GRAND AND CABINET PIANOFORTES;
FINE-TONED CHURCH ORGAN, by GREEN; AND A BARREL CHAMBER ORGAN;
An Elegant Range of Mahogany Library Wing Bookcases;
HANDSOME GILT CHASED OR-MOLU CANDELABRAS, GIRANDOLES, &c.;
MASSIVE SERVICE OF SILVER AND GILT PLATE,
NEAR NINE THOUSAND OUNCES;
CELLARS OF FINE OLD WINES, ABOUT 250 DOZEN;
BEAUTIFUL DAMASK LINEN; ELEGANT CHINA AND RICH CUT GLASS,
OF ALL DESCRIPTIONS;
VALUABLE LIBRARY OF BOOKS,
By the most esteemed Authors in every Branch of Literature;
CURIOUS AND UNIQUE MANUSCRIPTS ON VELLUM;
AN EXCELLENT SELENOGRAPHIA GLOBE, by RUSSELL;
FINE PAINTINGS,
By Eminent Masters, particularly a SPLENDID GALLERY PICTURE, by TOMASO MANZUOLI DI FRIANO, representing the Visit of the Virgin to her Cousin Elizabeth;
SUPERB SCULPTURES IN MARBLE,
Including the APOLLO BELVIDERE, by DEARE, 7-feet-6 high;
An Antique Circular Sarcophagus; a beautiful Unique Candelabrum, 8-feet-3 high: fine Statue of Esculapus;
BUST OF WILLIAM PITT, by NOLLEKENS;
BEAUTIFUL ANTIQUE ETRUSCAN, COLUMNAR, AND CAMPANA VASES; PRÆFERICULUMS; MIROPOLAS;
And other Specimens of Roman and Grecian Antiquities;
A MATCHLESS LARGE CORK MODEL OF MOUNT VESUVIUS,
By the celebrated Traveller, Dr. CLARKE;
COSTLY MAHOGANY GENTLEMAN'S TURNING LATHE,
DRILLING LATHE, AND VICE BENCH, ex suite;
GRINDING & POLISHING MACHINES, PORTABLE FORGE, &c., by HOLTZAPFEL & Co., London;
Tools, Cases, and Apparatus complete; and a variety of other Articles;
Which will be Sold by Auction,
BY MR. ROBINS,
OF WARWICK HOUSE, REGENT STREET,
AT THE MAGNIFICENT MANSION, ATTINGHAM HALL,
NEAR SHREWSBURY,
On MONDAY, the 30th of JULY, 1827, and FIFTEEN following DAYS,
(Saturdays and Sundays excepted), each Day precisely at Twelve o'Clock,
BY ORDER OF THE RIGHT HONOURABLE LORD BERWICK.
Mr. ROBINS informs the NOBILITY, GENTRY, and the PUBLIC, that the whole will be Sold without Reserve; and pledges himself that not a single Article is inserted in the Catalogues but the bonâ fide Property of his Lordship.
May be viewed on Monday, the 28th of May instant, until the time of Sale (Sundays excepted), by Catalogues, at TEN SHILLINGS each, which may be had at ATTINGHAM HALL; of Messrs. TENNANT, HARRISON, & TENNANT, Solicitors, Gray's Inn Square; Messrs. DUKES & SALT, Solicitors, Shrewsbury; and at Mr. ROBINS, No. 170, Regent Street, London.
PRINTED BY T. BRETTELL, RUPERT STREET, HAYMARKET, LONDON.

An Army of Servants?

From a servant's point of view, Attingham's heyday was during Thomas, 2nd Lord Berwick's time in the early 1800s.

Many hands

Attingham needed dozens of staff to keep the large mansion, stables, gardens and estate working smoothly and efficiently. Large retinues of staff at Attingham and the London houses demonstrated the Berwicks' power, social status and wealth. Accurate numbers are uncertain, because archive records are patchy, perhaps due to the fluctuating fortunes of the Berwicks. In any case, servant numbers changed constantly and varied during the year, depending upon whether the Berwicks were in residence or elsewhere. Noble families moved about a great deal and the 1st, 2nd and 3rd Lords Berwick divided their time between Shropshire and London. The Berwicks were usually at Attingham from Christmas to Easter and from August to mid-October. More staff were needed at these times and local people were recruited to help with the extra work.

A fair wage

Servants in a great house worked long days but they had a comparatively good lifestyle, certainly better than that of a servant of the middle or lower classes or an agricultural labourer. Their contract included breakfast, dinner, tea and supper with a beer or tea allowance. Uniforms were supplied and their wages, paid twice or four times a year, varied between £6 and £50 a year, according to the job in the early 1800s.

Perquisites or 'perks' were an acknowledged part of servants' wages. Footmen received tips for running errands and the butler could sell empty wine bottles, corks and candle ends. The cook sold bone, fat and dripping to local people and the scullery maid sold rabbit skins to visiting traders.

A strict hierarchy

The mansion is divided into a feminine and a masculine side. The servants' accommodation was also arranged in this way, and the staff were further divided into upper and lower servants, reflected by their dress and food. Upper servants such as the steward or land agent, butler, housekeeper and cook liaised with Lord and Lady Berwick about the running of the estate and household.

The lower servants seldom or never encountered his Lordship or her Ladyship as they were not allowed beyond the servants' area other than to perform their tasks. Lower servants would also work for upper servants. Upper servants ate dinner at midday in the Steward's or Housekeeper's Room, lower servants in the Servants' Hall. Men sat on one side of the table, women on the other, presided over by the head coachman and upper housemaid. Kitchen staff ate in the kitchen.

Opposite top When staying in Brighton, Thomas, 2nd Lord Berwick had apples sent down from Attingham

Opposite bottom Servant bells at Attingham

Right The hierarchy of domestic staff even applied at mealtimes, with upper and lower and kitchen staff eating in separate rooms

Working for Thomas, 2nd Lord Berwick

When Thomas inherited Attingham in 1789 it is likely he took on new servants. Although a bachelor at the time, the mansion often housed many family members and other guests. Thomas's house steward recorded over 20 family members resident on two occasions between 1801 and 1807, presenting the household staff with many demands on their time. His staff included a house steward and land agent who took charge of the mansion and the estate. He also had a personal valet, a butler and under butler, a housekeeper, cook, footmen and maids working in the house, kitchen, laundry, scullery and still-room. Outside there were coachmen, grooms, postillions and gamekeepers as well as gardeners. When Thomas married Sophia in 1812, more servants were employed, including a lady's maid and, from time to time, French chefs. Records also suggest that some work, such as laundry, was contracted out, possibly at busy times.

Right Attingham's heyday was during the time of Thomas, 2nd Lord Berwick in the early 1800s

A good employer?

Attingham's household records suggest that Thomas was a considerate employer. He paid coach fares for staff that were discharged from Attingham and also paid the medical bills of his staff and their families. In 1801/2 Thomas paid £21 for the apothecary's visits and tinctures of myrrh and magnesium for George Scoble, his valet, as well as medicines for the workmen and for the apothecary to attend the gardener's wife. Thomas seems to have paid wages that were comparable with other country estates. However there are records of servants being paid late, particularly in the mid-1820s when Thomas was heading for financial ruin. It was left to Elizabeth Early, the housekeeper, and Richard Partridge, the steward, to dismiss most of the household when the 1827 auction was held.

A class of their own

In the late 18th and early 19th centuries servants made up the largest occupational group in England. Even the lower classes might employ a maid. Large retinues of staff at Attingham and the London houses demonstrated the Berwicks' power, social status and wealth. This cartoon from 1805 shows a lord and lady in a 'Register Office for the Hiring of Servants'.

Travelling light

When Thomas travelled to London he would take some servants with him, such as the butler, footmen and kitchen maids as well as his 'plate' or silverware, kitchen equipment and boxes of goods. He paid for others to travel to London by stagecoach. Quite an adventure for a Shropshire servant.

Small beer

Beer was part of a servant's wages and they were paid the cash equivalent if they didn't want beer. In 1800 two of Thomas's maids were paid a guinea (one pound, one shilling) as their annual tea allowance because they didn't take beer. This was in addition to their annual wage of £8 1s 0d, paid quarterly.

All in a day's work

Mary Mann, still-room maid

Mary Mann worked at Attingham in 1826. Her position was relatively high on the house staff ladder, as she worked for the housekeeper, Elizabeth Early. Mary also travelled with Thomas, 2nd Lord Berwick, when he went up to his London house.

Early rising

Mary's day began at 6am, when she cleaned the housekeeper's rooms and lit the fires before helping with the Berwicks' breakfast trays. She worked for a few hours before breakfasting on bread and butter with jam and left-over cold meat.

Below The sugar-work and marzipan decorations for the dining-room table would have been created by a master confectioner

Pastries and potions

Mary's work included helping to check the inventories of household linen, crockery and utensils. She also made pastries, cakes, jams and pickles for the household as well as homemade remedies, perfumes and cosmetics for Lady Berwick.

Sweet treats

A still-room maid was one of the few staff allowed into the Still-room, where costly items such as tea and sugar were kept. Attingham's Still-room Kitchen is a rare example of a Georgian confectionery still retaining its specialist oven. An expert confectioner was occasionally brought to Attingham to make exotic and elaborate sugar-work desserts for the Berwicks' dinner parties.

Left Part of the copper *batterie de cuisine* in the main kitchen

Henry Faulkus, footman

As a footman at Attingham, Henry was 'on show' to the Berwicks and their guests, so he wore Attingham livery when he was serving tea, or waiting at dinner. He had 'drab' or work clothes for other tasks such as moving furniture, cleaning, polishing silver or carrying coals to the rooms.

Partial to tarts

Henry often accompanied Sophia, Lady Berwick, when she was out visiting or shopping. He paid for her purchases and alms she gave to poor people. In May 1819 Henry was reimbursed £1 os 4d for raspberry tarts, letters, flowers and the fare for a hackney coach as well as alms to a poor woman and a blind man.

'Calves before character'

Footmen were the principal servants on show and indicated the wealth and social standing of the Berwicks. Their looks and height were all important. It was often said that 'manly calves' were more important than a footman's reference or 'character' from previous employers.

Plate hands

Footmen's tasks included cleaning silver, known as 'plate'. This gave them 'plate hands' because they used jeweller's rouge mixed with ammonia (stale urine) to clean silver with their bare hands. Their hands bled and blistered before healing, leaving calluses and scars. For this reason footmen wore white gloves when on show.

'Flunky'

This was coined as a derogatory name for footmen. Footmen were often considered idle, as they did little or no manual labour and spent much of their time waiting around until their masters or mistresses needed them. At dinner footmen held diners' glasses, except when they were drinking, to prevent wine coming into contact with the expensive white tablecloth. After dinner they might be required to remove the gentlemen's chamber pots.

The last servants at Attingham

When Thomas and Teresa, the 8th Lord and Lady Berwick, arrived in Shropshire after their honeymoon, they initially lived at Cronkhill, the Italianate villa on the estate. The mansion was let to the wealthy Van Bergen family whose rent provided welcome income for Attingham. After reduced circumstances of previous generations, the finances of the estate were in a sorry state.

Thomas hoped to find new tenants but this proved impossible, due to the poor condition and large size of the mansion. So, in 1921 he and Teresa moved into Attingham, with just three or four staff, a far cry from the days of Thomas, 2nd Lord Berwick, who had dozens of servants in the early 1800s. Mrs Harris was the cook, and two brothers, Arthur and Harry Mullins, were the butler and caretaker. A few other members of staff were hired, such as Mr Rowe, the chauffeur. However, by the 1930s, the numbers of servants had been reduced due to the finances of the Berwicks.

Above Letters from Mrs Durward, Attingham's last housekeeper, to Teresa, Lady Berwick

Left The 8th Lord and Lady Berwick in 'Teresa's little Renault' with their chauffeur, Rowe, and two Alsatians

Staff relations

Mrs Durward was the last housekeeper at Attingham. These letters to the 8th Lady Berwick – addressed to 'My Lady' – show a warmth and affection born of a good relationship between employer and employee.

'Thank you very much for bringing me to the Station. I found my Sister quite well today. I am going down for tea with the children; it will be nice to see them.'

'I do hope you will keep better while you are away. You will feel the cold very much if the Club is nice and warm like Attingham and then go out.'

Above Female servants at Attingham in 1936. Mrs Lawley (far right) married one of the gardeners and they left not long afterwards

Letters home

Teresa wrote frequently to her mother, Costanza Hulton, about her plans for Attingham. Teresa's letters reveal the enormity of the task she had set herself. She described the east front rooms on the first floor as being 'in chaos'.

'Attingham is stuffed full of treasures of all kinds but at present the Van Bergens have made it hideous and covered up all the nice furniture.'

'It needs a tremendous lot doing, all the carpets worn out and the walls to my mind uglily painted.'

The Walled Garden and the Stables

The Walled Garden was the most intensively productive area of the estate. Here and at the Stables were the scenes of the greatest industry, the engine rooms of the estate. This long history of production continues to the present day.

Beauty and bounty

Attingham's walled garden and orchard were probably built at the same time as the mansion for Noel, 1st Lord Berwick, in the 1780s. As was usual for functional and productive Georgian gardens, it was located out of sight of the mansion, on slightly raised ground that was at less risk of flooding from the Severn.

The high walls around the garden created a warm, sheltered micro-climate for plants and protected the contents from theft. There are two areas of walled garden at Attingham: the main, almost rectangular area and an adjacent, smaller triangular area, which contains the frameyard with glasshouses and cold frames as well as the gardeners' bothy.

Pines and vines

Georgian gardeners were capable of growing pineapples and exotic grapes. Attingham has 'pineapple pits' which were heated by rotting manure and oak bark. With careful management it was possible to produce pineapples in the winter. Thomas Hill, the 1st Lord Berwick's father, wrote to his son in London asking if he wanted 'pines for the table at Christmas'.

Necessity and luxury

The kitchen garden was a vital element of every home, cottage and country estate alike, providing food throughout the year. Attingham's Walled Garden supplied the Berwicks, household staff and guests with a constant source of fruit, flowers, vegetables and honey. It was cleverly cultivated. Skilled gardeners extended the natural growing season by choosing early and late varieties of fruit and vegetables and by using heated walls and glasshouses and sophisticated storage. In this way they were able to produce luxuries such as grapes, melons and mushrooms most of the year round.

Careful planning

The gardeners had to provide food for wildly varying numbers of people. Sometimes it was just the family and household staff to supply, at other times the mansion was full of guests and their staff. The head gardener had to be aware of the Berwicks' social calendar and prepare accordingly.

No expense spared

Creating a large walled garden was an expensive business, requiring thousands of bricks or pieces of stone. Bricks were considered the best material and were the most expensive option. They make strong, dry walls that retain heat, and nails can easily be hammered into the mortar to support fruit trees. Attingham's Walled Garden is constructed entirely of brick; many other gardens had the outer walls made of cheaper stone or cob, a mix of sand, mud and straw.

Glass and frames

Other major expenses for Attingham's gardens were heating and glazing. The walls were heated by coal-fired furnaces which heated flues inside the walls to encourage tender plants and protect blossom from frost. The glazed garden frames and glasshouses were also heated to produce fruit whatever the season. Fortunately Attingham's gardeners had generous budgets – Noel Hill, 1st Lord Berwick, was persuaded to order large consignments of ornamental fruit trees in the 1770s from Williamson & Co., leading London nurserymen of the time.

Opposite The Walled Garden

Above Production has started again in the melon house

Below An invoice for Attingham's annual seed order in 1895

Garden design

Left Repton's 'business card', used as the frontispiece to the Red Book he produced for Attingham

Although the primary role of the Walled Garden was productivity, it was also a place of beauty, prowess and prestige, visited by the family and their guests for pleasure and leisure. When Humphry Repton was hired by Thomas, 2nd Lord Berwick, to enhance the grounds and parkland, he made recommendations in one of his famous Red Books to improve the approach to the Walled Garden, commenting that 'the walk to the kitchen garden will be greatly improved by doing away with some of its sameness and confinement'.

Elegant designs

The structure and layout of the Walled Garden was planned meticulously. The height of the substantial brick walls that surround the garden was scientifically calculated to create specific airflow patterns over the walls and inside the growing space. The walls were often the most productive area of the garden and every bit of space was used, with fruit trees grown against the walls, trained on wires into decorative shapes, known as espaliers.

Left Map from Repton's Red Book, 1797

Sheds and slips

The north walls have a cavity between the inner and outer walls which was heated to protect the fruit trees from frost. Sheds on the back of the north wall were used as root and apple stores and for growing mushrooms. Ground outside the south and west walls was also used for food production and known as the 'slip' gardens. Root vegetables and other crops which didn't need so much protection from wind were grown in the slips.

A fruitful orchard

The orchard has 160 trees and 37 different varieties of fruit trees. There are apples, damsons and walnuts growing here, many of them local varieties. They were chosen to provide fruit for the table almost all year round.

Regency bee house

One of the garden's treasures is the bee house, one of only two known Regency bee houses in the country. It was originally sited in the orchard to encourage pollination of the fruit trees, but was relocated to the lawn south of the Walled Garden. No one is certain who designed it but it could have been John Nash or Humphry Repton when they were working for Thomas, 2nd Lord Berwick, in the early 1800s. Today, the bees are kept in hives across the estate and there is a demonstration bee hive located in the orchard. The bees are looked after by the Attingham beekeeper and our volunteers.

Left Gardeners picking the organic fruit

Below left The 18th-century Grade II listed bee house is one of only two in the country

Below The Attingham orchard is a lovely spot for a picnic

Daily life in the Walled Garden

Kitchen gardens were busy, highly productive work spaces, with gardeners sowing, weeding, watering, harvesting and storing produce as well as planning future crops. Attingham's Walled Garden covers over 2.5 acres. Each acre was generally expected to produce food for twelve people and required two or three gardeners to look after it, so there were probably around eight gardeners in the Walled Garden when it was in full production in the late 1700s and early 1800s.

Outside and inside

The head gardener and his team controlled the garden, supplied the kitchen and arranged all the indoor flowers and any floral table decorations. 'Outside men' worked on the open ground and 'inside men' tended the glasshouses. Experienced, older gardeners lived on the estate, but unmarried lads slept in the bothy attic, near the boilers and glasshouse which needed tending day and night.

Water supplies

Water came from a well close to the dipping pool in the centre of the large garden. Water was lifted from the well in buckets and cans and stored in the dipping pool before it was taken to where it was needed. An old wheeled water carrier is still used in the garden today.

A well in the orchard supplied the small walled garden and the glasshouses, but has since been filled in. A concrete underground tank installed in the early 1900s to store water collected from the roofs of the glasshouses has been recently restored. A pump in the melon house brings this water to the garden and all the watering in the frame yard is done with rainwater.

Above A team of gardeners would have worked under the head gardener

Left The Walled Garden produced an abundance of flowers as well as food

'His Lordship was a kind and rather shy gentleman.... I remember him asking my boss, the head gardener, if he might pick up a windfall apricot.'

Mike Threadgold, July 2010.

Mike worked in the Walled Garden in the 1950s and 1960s.

Abandonment and revival

Like many formal kitchen gardens, Attingham's garden declined after the Second World War. England's social structure had changed irrevocably – the owners of many grand country houses couldn't afford to maintain them and many people who had worked there had gone to war. Attingham's time as an Adult Education College saw the Walled Garden grassed over to make a football field. In the early 1990s the National Trust planted Christmas trees in the garden as a cash crop. In the mid-1990s the National Trust began research to guide the future restoration of the garden. In 2008 one quarter of the garden returned to cultivation and since then the ambitious programme to restore it to full productivity has forged ahead.

Going local
The restoration of the Walled Garden began in 2008. The glasshouses and vinery have been repaired and the gardeners' bothy has been restored and is once more the head gardener's office as well as a demonstration potting area with information about the history of the Walled Garden. The restoration demonstrates the garden's crucial role not only to the household but also to the self-sufficiency of the estate. It also supports the National Trust's commitment to sustainability, organic cultivation and locally grown food. Visitors can see fruit and vegetables growing in the garden, eat them in the restaurant and tearooms and buy some to take home.

A productive future

Future plans for the Walled Garden echo the approach to the restoration and conservation work in the mansion. The back sheds are being restored and some original structures in the garden, such as the peach house, are being excavated. New facilities are bringing more life into the garden, and bees and hens have been reintroduced.

A rare Georgian kitchen garden

Attingham is an excellent example of a late 18th-century walled garden. Unusually, it wasn't 'modernised' during Victorian times, nor was it demolished during the 1950s and 1960s when many historic gardens were deemed economically unviable. The current restoration programme returns the garden to its original function, producing food and flowers for people at Attingham.

Left Attingham's fruit, vegetables and flowers are available to buy

Above The glasshouses and flowers in the frame yard

Opposite The Walled Garden is an area of peace and tranquillity

'I established an outlet for produce to the Officers' Mess on the RAF station and kept them supplied with fruit and vegetables … other produce was sold to shops in Shrewsbury, usually transported by Lady Berwick , or in her absence, I was trusted to take the boxes of produce into town in the Rover – the "poshest" car I had ever driven.'

Mary Gatecliff, Head Gardener, 1941–4

'When I started working in the Walled Garden in spring 2009, I was daunted by its massive scale: a huge two-acre site of earth, grass and walls. We've started to return the permanent planting to the gardens – espaliered pears in the beds, peaches, plums, nectarines and apples against the walls. Tying in the new growth on those trees gives me a wonderful sense of connection with generations of gardeners who worked here before me.'

Kate Nicoll, Walled Gardener, 2010

'An architectural statement in its own right'

Attingham's Georgian stables were designed by George Steuart for Noel Hill, 1st Lord Berwick, at the same time as the mansion, 1782–5. Built around a courtyard, they included stalls for 56 horses, tack rooms for saddles, bridles and harness, carriage houses as well as living space for the grooms, coachmen and stable boys. The gamekeeper kept hounds and ferrets here and game was hung in the game room to mature. The blacksmith's smithy and carpenter's workshops were also in the stable courtyard, making and repairing tools and equipment for the stables, the house and the estate.

Above Lord Berwick's race horse, 'Bishop' and a groom

Creating an impression

In the 1st, 2nd and 3rd Lord Berwick's time the brick walls of the stables were lime-washed a yellow-grey colour to give the impression that the whole building was made of expensive Grinshill stone, a high-quality, durable and attractive sandstone quarried at Clive, just north of Shrewsbury. Nationally recognised for its outstanding building qualities of strength and beauty, Grinshill stone was used at Worcester Cathedral, Powis Castle, Downing Street and Chequers.

All about location

The stables were a bustling place, noisy and smelly too, which is why they were built away from the mansion. As with the mansion, Attingham's stables were built to impress. Their grandeur, size and fine architectural detail demonstrated the status and wealth of the Berwicks, and the numbers of horses and staff they housed. Their prominent location, designed to be seen by visitors on their approach to the mansion and set within a designed landscape, is certainly impressive.

'The most splendid of all the estate buildings'

Attingham's stables were considered exceptional even in their day, and were included in the New Vitruvius Britannicus, an important 18th-century publication on architecture. Built of brick and faced with fine ashlar Grinshill stone on the main, southern side, the stables form a quadrangle enclosing a courtyard entered through tall archways. The internal fittings of Attingham's stables were graded according to the value of the horse. Lord Berwick's racehorses had the most luxurious stalls with curved dividing walls adorned with fluted urns. Other horses had less elaborate stables, but theirs were still spacious with glazed windows and grooved stone floors for good drainage.

Right For a functional building, the interior of the stables was highly ornamented

Horsepower and pleasure

Above Selena Noel Hill, sister of Richard, 7th Lord Berwick, in pony and trap

Left A hunt meet outside Attingham in the early 1920s

Hunting and horseracing were the 1st Lord Berwick's favourite country pastimes. However, horses weren't just a leisure interest – they were absolutely vital to everyday life and to the running of the estate as the main source of transport and communication for people and power for agriculture. The stables were a crucial part of any country estate, housing all the horses used by the family for riding or travelling in their carriages as well as horses that worked on the land.

Travelling around

Wealthy Georgian families travelled a surprising amount, and the Berwicks journeyed frequently between Attingham and their London houses as well as around Shropshire. They called on friends and neighbours, visited tenants and enjoyed going out to concerts, theatres and Shrewsbury Races as well as visiting popular towns and spas like Harrogate and Bath. The Berwicks' collection of coaches and carriages was kept in the stable courtyard, each designed for specific journeys. There were coaches and chariots for long distance travel, phaetons for fun and speed, soft tops for sunny days and light curricles, barouches and landaus for local visiting and shopping.

Matching pairs

Horses which pulled carriages were usually bought and sold as matching pairs. The better the match of the horses, the more expensive the horses. The Berwicks' coaches and carriages were impressive too, highly varnished and painted in the family colours, black and patent yellow, with the crest and coronet on the sides. The interior of a coach bought by Noel, 1st Lord Berwick, in 1783 was 'lined with yellow cloth trimmed with velvet lace … plate glasses and venetian blinds in the doors, wainscot trunks under the seats, double steps and a carpet in the bottom'. A phaeton, an informal pleasure coach, was sent to Naples in 1793, presumably for Thomas, 2nd Lord Berwick, who was on his Grand Tour at the time, at a cost of £190 12s od.

A gentleman's horse

Country pursuits such as hunting and racing were not only highly fashionable among wealthy landowners in the late 1700s, but were also considered virtuous pastimes. Nature was seen as a spiritual force, giving added meaning to life and a country gentleman on horseback was considered to be 'at one with nature'. Horses were of great importance to Noel, 1st Lord Berwick, who enjoyed horse racing and fox hunting. There is a painting in the Attingham collection which is believed to be of Noel Hill on horseback (below).

Above The 8th lord Berwick on horseback, early 1900s

Left Silver racing trophy won at Oswestry races in 1778

Attingham Park and Estate

Attingham has a rich and multi-layered archaeological landscape. The fertile valley of the River Severn has a long history of human activity and settlement.

People have lived here since at least the Bronze Age, around 4,000 years ago, farming the rich, alluvial soils and using the rivers for water, food and transport. There are seven Scheduled Ancient Monuments on the estate, including Iron Age settlements, two Saxon palaces, Roman forts and one third of the Roman city of Viroconium (now known as Wroxeter). There are also ancient crop marks, a medieval roadway, early toll roads and the sites of the 18th-century iron forges on the Tern that contributed to the 1st Lord Berwick's fortune.

Water power

The Severn and Tern rivers have always had an important role in Attingham's estate. Historically the Tern powered corn mills and iron forges, but they were closed by the 1st Lord Berwick's father in the 1750s because of their noise and pollution. The water meadows beside the rivers were, and still are, valuable for grazing and hay production, with sluices controlling water levels to encourage early and nutritious grass crops. The Severn is notorious for flooding and the water meadows and pastures offer useful water storage, as they have done for centuries.

The Berwicks' landscape

The Berwicks were only at Attingham for just over 200 years but their legacy in the landscape is impressive. They built the mansion, stables, walled garden and icehouses. Entrances and drives were improved, and the Deer Park created within a Repton-designed Picturesque landscape. Thousands of acres were brought into efficient agricultural production, farm buildings were altered and the routes of rivers and roads altered to suit the Berwicks' views. Further layers of history were added in the Second World War with an airfield, hospital and barracks on the estate. The National Trust is gradually revealing the hidden history of this intriguing landscape, nurturing its historic design and enhancing its biodiversity.

The view of the Shropshire Hills from the upper rooms of the house

The Attingham estate

Left British longhorn cattle at Attingham

Below Cronkhill on the Attingham estate; for opening hours, contact the National Trust at Attingham or visit www.nationaltrust.org.uk

Right Woodland is managed to balance the needs of visitors, the estate and of wildlife

Today the Attingham estate covers nearly 4,000 acres (around 1,500 hectares), about half its size in the early 1800s. Like all great country estates, Attingham's land has always played a vital role, providing not only food for the table and fuel for the fires but also income, a role that continues today.

As well as 400 acres of parkland, there are well over 300 acres of woodland, tenanted farms and properties, including Cronkhill, the architecturally important Italianate Regency villa designed and built in 1802 by John Nash as a Picturesque 'eye-catcher'. It is open to the public several days each year.

Buying it up, selling it off

The estate was managed by an estate steward or land agent, supervised by each Lord Berwick, some more actively than others. Noel Hill, 1st Lord Berwick, moved the old London to Holyhead road further away from the house and paid for the ornamentation on the new bridge. His son Thomas, 2nd Lord Berwick, significantly increased the estate in the early 1800s to around 8,000 acres. After the financial disaster brought on by Thomas and the sales of 1827 and 1829, it was left to his brother William, later 3rd Lord Berwick, to keep Attingham held together.

Revival and survival

The 5th Lord Berwick made improvements, building 'model farms' and developing one of the first, and finest, herds of Hereford cattle in England. Thomas, 8th Lord Berwick, carefully nurtured the estate during his lifetime with the help of his land agent, Gordon Miller. Although a significant acreage was mortgaged or sold, the productivity of the remaining land was increased and its woodlands and ancient trees protected during the Second World War, despite pressure to supply timber to the war effort. The sale of land funded the restoration of the mansion and secured the survival of the estate during the Great Depression of the 1930s.

Woods for life

Attingham estate includes 370 acres of woodland. Traditionally this provided the estate with timber for buildings, wood for carpentry, fencing, tools and household items. The National Trust continues working the woods for the estate's needs and sells charcoal and firewood. The Trust also manages the woodland for recreation and bio-diversity, creating rich habitats with many types of ancient and young trees, which, in turn, attract more plants and animals.

A living larder

Attingham's parkland is a landscape designed for pleasure and recreation. It was also carefully managed and highly functional, providing venison, pheasant and other game for the table as well as eels, salmon and other fish from the weirs on the rivers Severn and Tern. Food from the rivers, Deer Park and Walled Garden provided fine dining for the Berwicks and their guests. One particularly prized specimen caught in the river is now on display in the Steward's Room.

Then and now

Today the National Trust balances the need for recreation and conservation. Over 400,000 visitors walk in the park every year, and their needs and safety are crucial, as is the conservation of Repton's designed landscape and its very special ecology with veteran trees and rare invertebrates. In the early 1800s dozens of servants worked in the stable courtyard, the grounds and the Deer Park. Today around nine members of full-time staff look after the Walled Garden, Parkland and estate. They are aided by over 100 volunteers without whom the task would be impossible.

Grand designers: Thomas Leggett and Humphry Repton

In 1770, two years after his marriage to Anne, Noel Hill, 1st Lord Berwick, engaged Thomas Leggett to improve the parkland around Tern Hall, the original house at Attingham. Leggett improved the pleasure grounds near Tern Hall and created the Mile Walk, a loop walk still in use today, from the mansion alongside the River Tern, returning past the Walled Garden. Leggett's work involved huge amounts of earth movement, walling, ditching and tree planting. Around 20,000 trees were planted over three years, including native and exotic specimens and over 160 fruit trees. Leggett also created 'sunken fences' to keep cattle off the Pleasure Walk whilst offering uninterrupted views of the parkland. Soon after Leggett's work was completed, Noel commissioned George Steuart to build the vast new Georgian mansion around Tern Hall, which he called Attingham Hall.

A 'Picturesque' setting

Noel's son Thomas, 2nd Lord Berwick, commissioned Humphry Repton, one of the most influential landscape designers of the time, to enhance the park. Repton visited Attingham and produced one of his famous Red Books, in which he presented his proposals with a series of 'before' and 'after' watercolour sketches.

Top 'Before' view from Tern Bridge, plate V from Repton's Red Book

Bottom The 'after' view

A man-made landscape

Repton's designs aimed to reduce the raw 'newness' of the mansion and create a 'natural' landscape around it. He sought to match the stature of the mansion by increasing the sense of scale of the surrounding parkland. He widened the River Tern and removed some of Leggett's planting to create views and vistas of the Shropshire Hills and the Wrekin. Repton also planted new copses and created new and impressive entrances and approach drives to the mansion.

Top designers

Humphry Repton and John Nash were two of the most influential designers of their day, Repton famous for his picturesque landscapes and Nash celebrated for his architectural flair. Attingham has all the trademarks of their work – originality, creativity and vision. The two men were business associates, friends and rivals. They often worked together, Nash designing the buildings and Repton creating the surrounding landscape. Their work at Attingham greatly enhanced the mansion and parkland as well as their careers. Repton was the first to call himself a landscape gardener, marketing himself as 'an improver of the landscape' with over 400 commissions in his 30-year career. Nash became the Prince Regent's favourite architect, designing some of London's most famous features such as Regent's Park and Regent Street as well as remodelling the iconic Brighton Pavilion.

Right Shrubs and trees listed on bills from between 1770 and 1806 are being replanted in the Pleasure Grounds as part of the restoration work

Restoring the Pleasure Grounds

The Mile Walk area is a key feature of Attingham's Grade II* designed landscape and a rare surviving example of a late 18th century extended pleasure ground circuit. Over the years, Thomas Leggett's work had become hidden beneath later schemes. In 2016 a long-term project began which aims to restore lost features, such as, planting schemes, sunken fences and views across the parkland to the Wrekin (seen below in Repton's watercolour).

Park life

A love of deer

Thomas, 8th Lord Berwick, was particularly fond of the deer at Attingham and fed them daily, with special favourites eating from his hand. He found the annual cull deeply distressing, and while appreciating its necessity, couldn't bear to be at Attingham when it happened, and usually visited London while the deed was done. Following his wishes, his ashes, and those of Teresa, his wife, were placed at the memorial in the Deer Park, in a glade with views of the estate, with the following inscription: 'His life added distinction to an honoured name; a generous and careful landlord, a patron and lover of the Arts, he studied to leave his inheritance a thing of beauty that posterity might enjoy'.

Attingham's Deer Park was created in 1798 as part of Thomas, 2nd Lord Berwick's grand improvements to the mansion and grounds. Wild fallow deer were already living in the estate's woodland and fields, and about 400 acres were fenced to create the Deer Park. The semi-wild deer in the park today are direct descendants of the deer owned by Thomas. In the 18th century, deer parks were fashionable status symbols, demonstrating the noble leisure interests of their wealthy owners. They also provided venison for the household. Today around 180 fallow deer live in the park, their numbers and overall health maintained by an annual cull in the winter months. The venison is still used to feed visitors to Attingham, being sold in the shop and served in the tearooms.

Great and small

Attingham's parkland is one of the richest and most important nature conservation sites for veteran trees and invertebrates in England. It has been designated a Site of Special Scientific Interest by Natural England. It is home to huge numbers of invertebrates, particularly the rare beetles that feed on and live in the trees and the dead and fallen branches. Attingham's oldest tree is nearly 700 years old and there are several others about 500 years old. These trees are carefully managed, balancing safe visitor access with maintaining the essence of Repton's landscape, all the time enhancing its bio-diversity.

Above Attingham's fallow deer have pale coats, known as 'menil'

Right The view over the pond towards the house

Wildlife

Changes and improvements in agriculture since the 1950s have had a profound impact on Attingham's farmland. As machinery got bigger and more powerful, fields were enlarged and hedges removed. Ponds were filled in and meadows and pastures ploughed up for arable crops or re-seeded which reduced the habitats for wildlife. Fortunately, the parkland around the mansion remained protected from these changes, remaining an oasis for wildlife, its value recognised by its designation as a Site of Special Scientific Interest and Grade 1 listing on English Heritage's Register of Parks and Gardens.

A central core

Today the rich parkland is the core from which wildlife can spread out across the estate. The National Trust works with farm tenants restoring hedges and ponds and re-creating riverside pastures full of grasses and wildflowers, spreading the bio-diversity at the heart of the estate to all parts.

A chance find
When new surfacing was needed for the paths to the Walled Garden in 2009, the ideal source of material was found, by chance, in the adjacent field where a pond was being renovated. Archaeological excavation revealed that the pond was man-made, lined with clay and had a big lead plug for regular cleaning out. Beneath the clay lay sands, gravels and pebbles that were ideal to re-make the paths. Hoggin, a mix of sand, gravel and pebbles, was traditionally used to surface paths and driveways. Pebbles aid drainage and the sand and grits gradually compact as people, horses and machinery use the surface. Many of the paths laid during the Berwicks' early days at Attingham were made of hoggin from the estate. The pond was probably originally a quarry for path materials in the 1st Lord Berwick's time.

Productive and sustainable

Attingham's land has always been productive, growing thousands of tons of crops on its rich soils. Today these crops include wheat, barley, oats and root vegetables. Organic dairy and beef plus timber and wood are also Attingham products. The National Trust works closely with its tenant farmers to ensure both productivity and sustainability. Since 2000 over 100 acres of riverside arable land have been returned to pasture, reducing the volume of soil swept into the river by rain and floods. Now there are three miles of bankside pastures along the rivers Tern and Severn, as there were when the 2nd Lord Berwick owned the land.

Encouraging wildlife

There is a huge variety of wildlife on the estate. Otters, salmon, kingfishers and sand martins visit the rivers, and the parkland trees. Woodland and estate buildings are home to all three kinds of woodpecker as well as nine different species of bat, numerous insects and other invertebrates. England's largest monitored breeding colony of pipistrelle bats live in the roof of one of the estate cottages. Fields and meadows are visited by hunting owls and buzzards and hares are often seen in the arable fields, which are managed to attract declining farmland birds such as grey partridge, skylark and lapwing, as well as for food production.

Above The River Tern flows through the Attingham estate and into the River Severn

Opposite Organic farming encourages wildflowers. Otters, kingfishers, dragonflies and pipistrelle bats are just some of the wildlife to be found on the estate

Attingham Re-discovered

The work that the 8th Lord and Lady Berwick began in the 1920s to conserve and restore Attingham is being continued by the National Trust today. Attingham Re-discovered is a long-term programme of conservation and restoration. The project began in 2000 with major work taking place from 2006.

Time for change

For nearly 50 years, until the late 1990s, only a fraction of Attingham's rooms were open to the public. Research revealed that visitors found the mansion forbidding, intimidating and dull. The Attingham Re-discovered project was set up to bring the house back to life, open new spaces, draw out the key layers of history and showcase conservation skills. Project work has taken place throughout many rooms in the house and has given people reasons to return to see the progress.

A new approach

What the project did differently was to carry out conservation-in-action in full view of the public, rather than behind closed doors. Even more than this, Attingham Re-discovered broke new ground in engaging visitors with the details, skills, dilemmas and cost of conservation. It was one of the first conservation projects to actively invite visitors to join in the debates and discussions of the project team.

Opposite The 8th Lord and Lady Berwick on the stairs at the front of the mansion, 1928

Below Conservators working on the collection

'The thought and trouble my husband and I took in trying to bring out the beauty of the old treasures here made them doubly dear to us. We only achieved a small part of what should have been done, but some day others will finish what we could not.'

From Lady Berwick's 1951 article in *The Townswoman* magazine.

Rolling out the red carpet

Left Careful cleaning and restoration took place at high level

Attingham Re-discovered goes through the roof

In 2012 the largest part of the project began. The Picture Gallery roof had leaked since it was first built by John Nash in 1805. The secondary roof, added over the top by the National Trust in 1974, was starting to fail and plans were drawn up for new glazing to protect the original roof and the precious contents of the gallery below. It took two years to remove the 1974 roof and install its 20 tonne replacement at a cost of £1.4 million to Attingham. Whilst this work was taking place, the interiors of the Picture Gallery were cleaned and restored over a period of three years.

The Picture Gallery carpet

Replacing the carpet in Nash's splendid Picture Gallery was the first major project. Research confirmed that his Regency design included crimson carpeting. The carpet that had been laid in 1994 was blue. After much consultation, a new crimson one, exactly matched to 19th-century fragments, was commissioned and made in Kidderminster. This was a huge undertaking which involved about four years of research, trials and consultation, dozens of specialists and a team of ten to install it.

Far left The new Picture Gallery carpet being laid

Left Each pane of glass for the new Picture Gallery roof was lifted over the mansion by a large crane

Opposite The Picture Gallery was created in 1805–7 by John Nash for Thomas, 2nd Lord Berwick

Bringing the house back to life

Conserving the Boudoir

The Boudoir was designed by Steuart as the innermost sanctuary in the feminine, eastern side of the mansion. It was designed for Anne, 1st Lady Berwick, with the theme of love depicted in gilded and painted cupids on the walls and ceiling. Over the two intervening centuries, the decoration had become darkened with dust, dirt and soot. After careful trials, the walls and ceiling were slowly and painstakingly cleaned by a painting conservator using cotton wool, deionised water and specialist detergent.

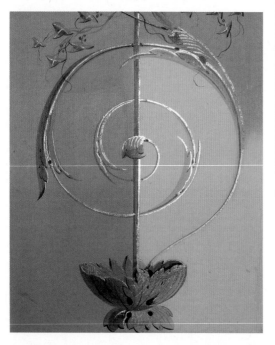

'What we thought was the patina of age was sheer dirt! The walls and ceiling of the Boudoir glow now…. it's a delight.'

Catriona Hughes, Conservator, 2010

Above and left The original, feminine decoration of the Boudoir now conserved but preserving a discreet, uncleaned area (top left) to show the difference

Restoring the Octagon Room

The Octagon Room is the climax of the masculine side of the mansion, balancing the Boudoir on the feminine side. Until recently people were unaware of the impact this room would have had in the early 1800s as Thomas, 2nd Lord Berwick's study. It had been completely redecorated in the 1970s, during the time of the Adult Education College. Paint analysis revealed dramatic Regency decoration of black and red graining. Research into textiles built up a picture of riotous colours including pink striped silk curtains lined with orange glazed wool, red leather upholstery and a blue and crimson carpet.

Below The vision for the restoration of the Regency scheme in the Octagon Room. Watercolour by Peter Brears, 2007

Conservation or restoration?

One of the first decisions is whether to conserve or restore. Conservation is always the primary aim, to stabilise the original item in its existing form. It's often more expensive than restoration, because it involves slow and labour-intensive work, but it ensures the survival of the original. Sometimes conservation just isn't possible – either because there's not enough evidence of the original or the damage can't be repaired. At Attingham, the original late 18th-century decoration in the Boudoir has been conserved, whereas the vibrant Regency scheme in the Octagon Room has been restored by re-creating paintwork and textiles.

'The Attingham Re-discovered Project puts the slow and painstaking processes of conservation work in front of our visitors and draws them into its fascinating micro-world of mixing rabbit-skin glue, taking chandeliers apart piece by piece and cleaning delicate decorative schemes over months with cotton wool buds.'

Sarah Kay, Curator, 2010

Attention to detail

Off the wall

Intriguing clues to a hidden decorative scheme on the upper flights of stairs and first floor corridors, led to ten years of analysis, investigation, consultation and trials before conservators were ready to start restoration. Six layers of oil paint were meticulously removed to reveal the 1807 distemper scheme on sheets of hand-made paper. The scheme was conserved where it survived and re-created where it did not.

'To have the possibility of removing many layers of oil-based over-paint from delicate distemper painted onto any surface is rare; to be able to successfully remove it from distemper painted onto *paper* is exceptional.'

Mark Sandiford, Conservator, 2009

Above A watercolour of the Dining Room, about 1840, by Lady Hester Leeke

Opposite The Dining Room table laid for a formal dinner

Right The miracle of removing layers of paint to reveal the original scheme

The Diplomat's Dinner

The Attingham Re-discovered Project has created a staggering display of an 1830s dinner in the Dining Room, combining important collections belonging to the 3rd Lord Berwick. Candlelight shimmers on his French porcelain dessert service, and is reflected on the mirrors of his ormolu (referring to the gilding process) table centrepieces. The elaborately arranged dessert and table decoration follows recipes and designs from The Italian Confectioner by G. A. Jarrin, published in 1827. All the table decorations – swans, temples, obelisks, flowers and butterflies – would have been edible, carefully modelled in sugar paste and marzipan.

Next steps

Involving visitors

Attingham Re-discovered is an ambitious long-term programme of conservation, restoration and re-creation. New work is being undertaken by the National Trust all the time and more is planned.

The project's active involvement of visitors has proved so popular and successful in the mansion that the same approach is being rolled out across the property. As the Walled Garden is gradually being brought back to life, choices need to be made between historical accuracy and maximum productivity. Other decisions involve the restoration of parkland features created by Thomas Leggett and Humphry Repton alongside the conservation of the parkland's rare and special wildlife. It's a crucial and delicate balancing act.

Sharing the passion

As well as witnessing subtle and significant physical changes, visitors enjoy talking to volunteers. They are Attingham's best ambassadors, sharing their passion and knowledge, telling the stories of this great Georgian country estate and the excitement and challenges at Attingham in the 21st century.

Below Volunteers in costume ready to welcome visitors to Attingham